LIVING ON STOLEN LAND

LIVING ON STOLEN LAND

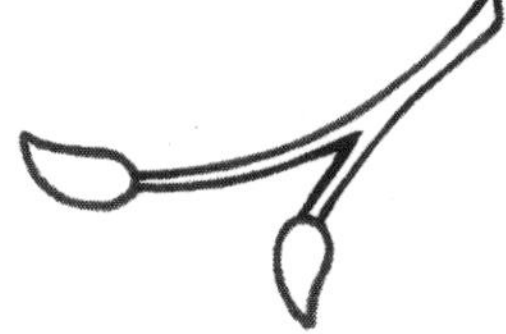

Ambelin Kwaymullina

This is a Magabala Book

Leading Publisher of Aboriginal and Torres Strait Islander Storytellers.

Changing the World, One Story at a Time.

First published 2020. Reprinted 2020 x2, 2021, 2022, 2023 x2, 2025
Magabala Books Aboriginal Corporation
1 Bagot Street, Broome, Western Australia
Website: www.magabala.com
Email: sales@magabala.com

Magabala Books receives financial assistance from the Commonwealth Government through the Australia Council, its arts advisory body. The State of Western Australia has made an investment in this project through the Department of Local Government, Sport and Cultural Industries. Magabala Books would like to acknowledge the generous support of the Shire of Broome, Western Australia.

Magabala Books is Australia's only independent Aboriginal and Torres Strait Islander publishing house. Magabala acknowledges the Traditional Owners of the Country of our many Nations. We recognise the unbroken connection to lands, waters and cultures. Through what we publish, we honour all our Elders, peoples and stories, past, present and future.

Cover Image Ambelin Kwaymullina
Cover Design Jo Hunt
Typeset by Jo Hunt
Printed and bound by Griffin Press, South Australia

ISBN (Print) 978-1-925936-24-7
ISBN (ePUB) 978-1-925936-26-1
ISBN (ePDF) 978-1-925936-25-4

Cataloguing-in-Publication data available from the National Library of Australia

A catalogue record for this book is available from the National Library of Australia

This story begins
with the tree on the cover
which shows futures

The roots go deep
down into the ground
because just futures
must be grounded in respectful relationships
with Indigenous peoples
Indigenous homelands
Indigenous sovereignties

The trunk
is the structures needed
for change
these include external structures
like just laws
policies
decision-making processes
but also
internal structures
of minds and hearts
patterns of thought and behaviour
towards Indigenous peoples

The leaves and flowers
are all the ideas
growth
possibilities
that will come

out of respectful relationships
and respectful structures
which will endure
for as long as the tree endures
for as long as it is cared for

YOU ARE
ON
INDIGENOUS
LAND

Stolen Land

You are on Indigenous lands
swimming in Indigenous waters
looking up at Indigenous skies

There is no part of this place
that was not
is not
cared for
loved
by an Aboriginal or Torres Strait Islander nation
There are no trees
rivers
hills
stars
that were not
are not
someone's kin

Those who are not Indigenous to this land
are Settlers
This does not mean
being a part of peaceful settlement
It means
being a part of settler-colonialism
a form of colonisation
where invaders came
and never left
Not like the places
where the colonising nation-states of Western Europe
established outposts

upended ancient governance structures
oppressed the peoples
stripped the land of wealth
but ultimately
went away

In settler-colonial places
like those
that Settlers named Australia
New Zealand
Canada
United States of America
Settlers never went away
Instead they sought
to permanently replace
Indigenous worlds with their own

For Aboriginal and Torres Strait Islander peoples
Settler arrival was an apocalypse
that repeated
each time Settlers reached
another Indigenous nation
The story of settler-colonisation
is the story of many apocalypses
storms of cataclysmic violence
erupting across
Indigenous homelands
relationships
families
lives

The chaotic violence
of these frontier apocalypses
was followed by the structured violence
of protectionism dystopias
where governments
stole children
kept files
policed every aspect
of Indigenous existence
sought to wipe out Indigenous languages
cultures
to make Indigenous peoples
like Settlers
albeit second-class ones
Then only the Settler world would exist
and there could be no challenge
to the Settler right to belong
No reminder
that the land belonged
to someone else

But the enterprise of annihilation
foundered on the rocks
of Indigenous resistance
which like the ancient stone
embedded in many Indigenous nations
flows from the heart of the earth
with only the tip appearing
above the surface
Settlers underestimated

the strength
the depth
the stubborn endurance
of Indigenous peoples
as we resisted in ways seen
and ways unseen

Two different worlds now exist
in the same space
and there is no place of innocence
for Settlers to stand
Not one location
where Settlers do not benefit
do not inherit the benefits
of the violent dispossession
of those who were here before

You are living on stolen land
What can you do about it?

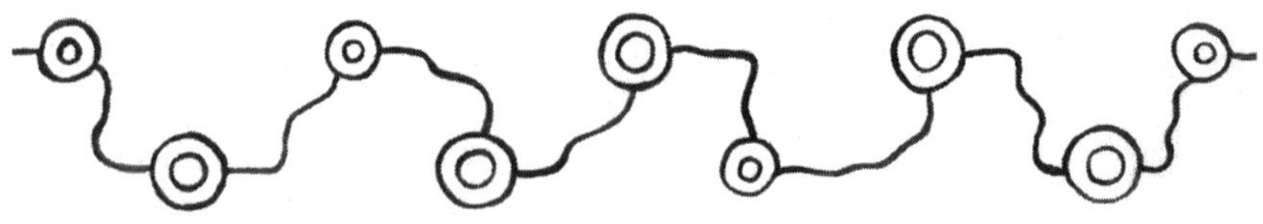

Sovereignties

There is not one Indigenous sovereignty
there are many
all the Aboriginal and Torres Strait Islander nations
are sovereign in their own homelands
Aboriginal people
name these homelands
our Countries

Indigenous sovereignties
are narrative sovereignties
they began and continue in story
the tales of the Ancestors
which tell of a world
that is alive

Everything has language
culture
law
Human beings
might not speak the language
of other forms of life
might not know
their law
all their culture-ways
but this does not mean
those ways do not exist
or that other life
is not family

Indigenous kinship systems
embrace all life in Country
everything is connected
related
and has a part to play
in holding up the world
Many of the first Settlers
saw kangaroos
as vermin
a species to be eradicated
Indigenous peoples knew
that kangaroos
shift the soil
help seeds to grow
this is part
of how kangaroo looks after Country

Within Indigenous systems
to be a fully realised individual
is to be part of a collective
and to live in a way
that ensures all other life
has the same opportunity
for self-realisation
so that all life
can speak their languages
follow their law
live their culture-ways
fulfil their role
of caring for Country

Loss of species
is loss of knowledge
that keeps the world turning

Among the questions
that systems founded in narrative sovereignties
asks any other system
that tries to claim the same space
are these:
What are your stories?
Where is your understanding
of life in Country
the connections that must be sustained
through the daily participation in
and management of
the sets of relationships
that the Ancestors established?

Settler systems
did not require stories like these
to claim sovereignty
Instead settler-colonialism
asserted a right
over inhabited lands
on the basis of the denigration
of those who live there
In Australia
this denigration
was expressed through *terra nullius*
the idea

that Australia was 'empty'
because First Peoples were not sufficiently 'civilised'
which is to say
our ways were not like the ways of the West

The assertion of right
is followed by the application of violence
through the apocalypses and dystopias
without which the land could not be taken
held
worked

The denigration
justified the violence
enabled it
that is why the denigration
is so necessary
so embedded
in settler-colonial nation-states
why it lingers
even after Settlers know it to be false
Without it
there is only the uncomfortable truth
that there was no justification
for what was done
no civilising mission
no manifest destiny
Just a land grab

The question remains
what is the basis
for the Settler claim of belonging
to Indigenous lands
waters
skies?
Where are the Settler stories
of relationships?
The ones that tell
of how Settlers
have respected Indigenous sovereignties
have walked humbly amongst Indigenous peoples
have respected Indigenous knowledges
and learned
how to hold up the connections
that are the world

And if there are no such Settler stories
or if there are not enough
then what are the pathways
by which such tales
can be created?

Time

Linear time
is something Settlers brought here
A version of time
that creates distance
Things that happened
a hundred years ago
are further away
than things that happened yesterday

A version of time
weaponised against Indigenous peoples
Our life ways
called 'backward'
of the past not of the future
Our Countries
described as 'new'
and newly discovered
despite being known and loved
for thousands of years
The history
of this ancient land
said to 'begin'
when Settlers arrived

A version of time
that is always carrying people away
from an unchangeable past
into an unknowable future
Giving the illusion of progress

regardless of whether
anything has changed

In Indigenous systems
time is not linear
It moves in cycles
It exists in space
in Country
and is as susceptible
to action and interaction
as any other life

On such a view
the ticking of clocks
the turning of calendars
makes nothing happen
moves nothing closer
or further away
from anything else
How far we have come
from the apocalypses and dystopias
of settler-colonialism
is measured by the degree
to which affected relationships
have been brought into balance
have been healed

To think of time in this way
is a gift
and a responsibility

It is a responsibility
because individual actions matter powerfully
radiating out
across all that would be thought of
in a linear sense
as past
present
future

It is a gift
because linear years
have never moved anyone so far
that meaningful action cannot be taken
to address the wounds
of settler-colonialism
The chance has not been lost
for justice
for change

Life doesn't move through time
Time moves through life

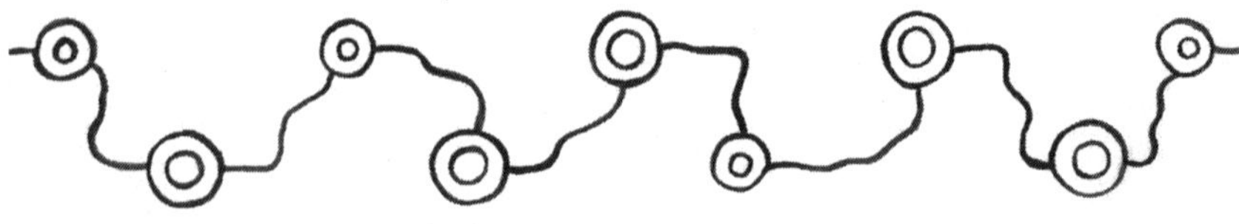

Decolonisation

Settler-colonial lands
will only be decolonised
when the structures of settler-colonialism
have been replaced
by structures grown out of respectful relationships
with Indigenous sovereignties

The structures of settler-colonialism
are everywhere
in governments
corporations
educational institutions
in every place
where something was founded
developed
sustained
in the absence of respect
for Indigenous sovereignties
These structures also exist
within Settlers
in the form
of patterns of thought
and behaviour

Decolonisation requires
that Settlers
continually identify
challenge
disrupt
the structures of settler-colonialism

including those patterns embedded
in minds and hearts
and in ways of relating
to Indigenous peoples

Decolonisation
is processes
It is journeys
not destinations
A series of transformations
which can only be born out of
and be answerable to
locally based relationships
with the sovereign Indigenous peoples
in whose homelands
Settlers live
work
play

PERSPECTIVES

Principles

Indigenous peoples
have many differences between us
but also commonalities
including that our systems
are holistic
process-focussed
and our knowledge
comes from connections

But the ways in which
these underlying ideas
these principles
are understood
applied
negotiated
is not the same
across different Indigenous contexts

It is important
to understand the difference
between principle and practice
For example
across all Indigenous homelands
there is the fundamental reciprocity
that if you care for Country
Country will care for you
But how Indigenous peoples care for homelands
and how those homelands care for us
changes
between different nations

Desert Country
is different to Sea Country
Sea Country
is different to Rangelands Country

We are many diverse nations
and context shapes meaning

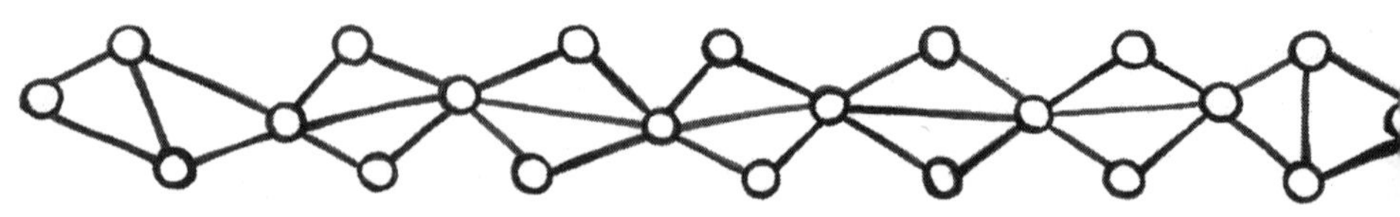

Holism

There is a pattern
made up of many threads
always moving
always changing
as the threads reach out
connect with each other
stretch across dimensions

The threads
are the shapes of life
that make up Country
tree
kangaroo
rock
river
human
hill
sun
moon
wind
and all the rest
The threads together
form the pattern
and the pattern
is in every thread

This way of thinking
that the whole is more
than its parts
and the whole is in all its

parts
is holistic
It is very different
to the thinking brought here
by the first Settlers
who arrived in an era
when Western thought-ways
were heavily influenced
by the reductionist idea
that the whole is never more
than the sum of its measurable parts

These different thought-ways
led to different views
of the same space
For example
ask a Settler reductionist thinker
to explain a hill
and they might speak
about its height
about the composition
of the rocks that form it
about the first Settler
to reach the peak
or to 'discover'
a hill that had been known about
and loved
for thousands of years

Ask an Indigenous thinker
to explain a hill
they might speak
about the river that runs past it
the plants and animals
to whom it is home
about the earth below
the turning stars above
about the Ancestor
who is the hill
the Ancestor hill
who is family

All parts of Country
must be respected
cared for
connected with
celebrated
to sustain the whole
that sustains us

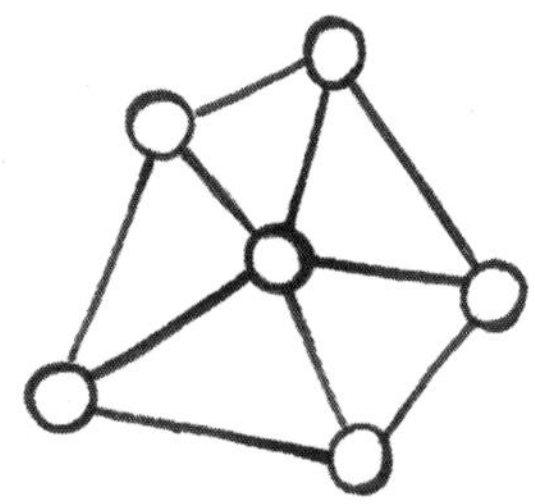

Processes

There is nothing inevitable
about what is
Life exists
because the Ancestors created it
through movement
through process
Life continues
because of the processes
which support it
all the ways
of caring for Country

Many Settler processes
are things of calendars
and ticking clocks
often demanding
an Indigenous response
by a certain date
within a certain time
impatient to get support
for an outcome
said to be good for Indigenous peoples
But what is the outcome really?
If it is something
that is supposed to support us
nurture us
or Country
then the process
by which it's achieved
must also support us

support Country
support Indigenous processes
which are of relationships
Date and time
is not important
what matters
is the making of connections
this is what moves things along

What is to be
does not exist
cannot exist
separate to the processes
that create it
the things we do
to reach an outcome
are the outcome
Like all things
process
must embody the whole
to support the whole

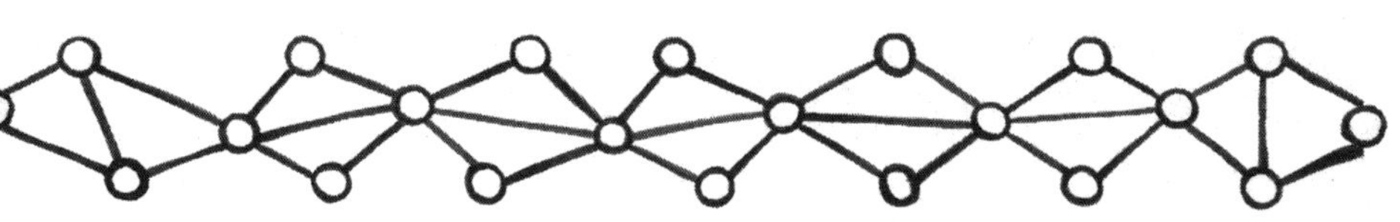

Knowing

In Indigenous systems
knowing
comes from understanding
how we connect
to all the life around us
and how all the life around us
connects to each other

Knowing
means understanding
there are things we can never know
All knowledge
is limited by positionality
and governed by relationships
The world
cannot be fully understood
by life in human shapes
because humans
cannot occupy the spaces held
by all other life
or see to the end of connections
Every pebble
contains the hill
but the hill
is greater than all the pebbles

This means
it is important to be cautious
about drawing conclusions
or setting yourself

on a course of action
Important
to be open to changing
to shifting
in response to shifts
in Country
Important
to maintain
constant awareness
of all the voices
of the life around you
and what
they're trying to tell you
One of my grandfathers called this
learning to read the signs

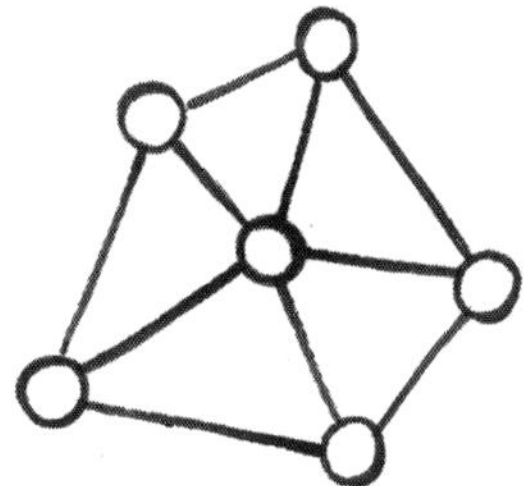

THE
LONG CON

Settler-colonialism

Settler-colonialism
is a long con
selling the lie
that taking living land by force
creates connection
creates belonging

Like all cons
settler-colonialism
puts on a show
dazzles with its achievements
the long march of its history
except
that march is short
merely a few steps
compared to the thousands of seasons
for which Indigenous peoples
have loved their lands

But settler-colonialism
doesn't tell that story
or if it does
it is only a preface
to what comes next
Settler histories
of brave pioneers
wealth and success
generated under difficult conditions
with no mention
of how much of that wealth

that success
relied on Indigenous knowledge
Indigenous ingenuity
on generations
of enslaved
indentured
Indigenous labour

Like all cons
settler-colonialism
denies its own nature
pretends lies are truths
gaslights anyone
who begins to suspect
all is not as it seems

Like all cons
when it is challenged
exposed
known for what it is
settler-colonialism
begins to lose
its power

The artificial context

Most of what Settlers know
about Indigenous peoples
is wrong
And it is wrong
in two ways

First
much of the information
Settlers have learned
or absorbed
without even realising
it was sinking into hearts and minds
is inaccurate
incomplete

But also
how Settlers know things
about Indigenous peoples
is wrong
because the knowledge is being processed
through an artificial context
which means
that even when Settlers hear
the voices of Indigenous peoples
speaking of our lives
our truths
there is a danger
of misconstruing
misinterpreting

misapplying
misappropriating

The artificial context
arises from the long con
of settler-colonialism
From the denigration of Indigenous peoples
as 'less than'
which has formed
the dominant environment
through which laws
policies
behaviours
attitudes
about Indigenous peoples
have been shaped
for almost all of the existence
of the settler-colonial state
called Australia

This context is artificial
because it is a lie
that Indigenous peoples are 'less than'
and because it denies the importance
of different ways of knowing and being
Claiming
that only knowledge-ways
law-ways
landholding-ways

like those of the West
have value

There are many Settlers
who oppose this context
as untrue
unjust
but to the extent
that it has become normalised
naturalised
its influence on Settler thoughts and behaviours
cannot be avoided
To believe it can be
is to fall for one of the tricks
by which the long con
sustains itself
and escapes justice

What you can do
is challenge it
by identifying wherever it appears
both within yourself
and outside yourself
This is part of what it means
to engage in
decolonising processes

Bias

Bias
comes in three forms
structural
explicit
unconscious

Structural bias
is found
in the ways in which
structures exclude
discriminate
at institutional
or systemic levels
such as
systemic racism

Structural bias
is in the laws
which disproportionately
negatively
impact on Indigenous peoples
It is in the circumstances
cultures
not taken into account
In the services not provided
or provided
to a lesser standard

Individuals benefit
from structural bias
through privilege
and while the most powerful form
of Settler privilege
is White privilege
all Settlers are privileged
in relation to Indigenous peoples
because all Settlers
benefit from Indigenous dispossession

Explicit bias
is in such things
as the denial of a job
the refusal to rent a house
to an Indigenous person
because they are Indigenous

When people say
'I'm not racist'
all they usually mean
is they don't hold
explicit bias
It does not mean
they are not the beneficiary
of structural bias
It does not mean
they are not influenced by
unconscious bias
It cannot mean this

because in a settler-colonial land
it is impossible
not to benefit from structural bias
not to hold unconscious bias
against Indigenous peoples

Unconscious bias
is different from explicit bias
because those who hold explicit bias
know they believe
that Indigenous peoples
are 'less than'
They might not say it
unless certain they are in the company
of like-minded people
but inside their own minds
they know
that is what
explicit bias
is

But unconscious bias
is bias that is held
but not known about
Unconscious bias
is the artificial context
of settler-colonialism
embedded deep
inside Settler minds

Explicit
unconscious
and structural bias
are not separate entities
They work together
reinforce each other
and have a cost
which is measured
in Indigenous pain
and in the worst of circumstances
in Indigenous lives

To fight
explicit bias
it must be named
for what it is
called out
every time it is encountered
as unacceptable
wrong

To fight
structural bias
it must be identified
not by reference to the good intentions
of the people who created
or work within the structures
but to the effects of the structures
the impacts
on Indigenous peoples

Structural bias
requires change
at systemic levels

Unconscious bias
can be the most difficult
to shift
because it is the best
at hiding
Many people think
that because they don't want to discriminate
they are incapable of doing so
But that is not how bias works
The only way
to not be the person who excludes
Is to know
you could be that person
Understanding that unconscious bias exists
means you will take steps
to check your bias
to prevent it
from manifesting in behaviours
and to begin
to change consciousness

The artificial context
was born from
sustained by
stories Settlers told
about Indigenous peoples

This means
one of the ways
to start to shift bias
is to engage with the
stories
that Indigenous peoples
tell about ourselves

Seek out the works
of Indigenous authors
playwrights
dancers
singers
Elders
communities
Not one story
not two
all of them
It will take
hundreds of stories
many years of listening
to create change

Behaviours

There are four sets
of common Settler behaviours
towards Indigenous peoples
at least
three are common
the fourth set
are emerging behaviours
for a changing world

First
are the people who talk
about their love
for Indigenous peoples
their commitment
to social justice
but who never
take any action

Do-nothing people
will waste the time
sap the energy
of anyone seeking change
through endless conversations
that lead nowhere
But they won't actively oppose
justice
they may even
give a little money
a little support
provided

it doesn't inconvenience them
too greatly
and they are assured
their contribution will be acknowledged

This means
do-nothing behaviours
are less toxic
than the next set
The behaviours
of saviourism

Saviours
have come to rescue Indigenous peoples
but they have no true interest
in decolonisation
because if Indigenous peoples
were no longer excluded
there would be nothing
for saviours to do
no one to save

Any ethical advocate
should seek
to make themselves redundant
Saviours work
to make themselves indispensable
They will only support Indigenous peoples
only capacity build
to the extent

that it doesn't threaten
their position

Saviours
work according to feelings
not standards
according to ideology
not evidence
They can speak
in superficial ways
of settler-colonialism
but cannot meaningfully
interrogate the ways
it informs their existence
and behaviour
Doing so
runs the danger
of identifying their own complicity
and saviours
are deeply invested
in their identities
as 'good Settlers'

Saviours
cannot yield space
They like to be centre stage
claiming responsibility
for any Indigenous success
expecting Indigenous peoples
to be grateful

for being saved
by a Settler
from the structures
behaviours
attitudes
that Settlers create
sustain
benefit from

The third set of behaviours
is the discoverers
who enact modern-day versions
of discovery doctrine
under which territory belonged
not to those who lived there
but to the first Christian Western European nation
to 'discover'
someone else's land

Discoverers
behave as if Indigenous worlds
only have meaning
only exist
when known to
and misappropriated by
a Settler
They talk a lot
about Indigenous peoples
or rather
they talk about the part

that Indigenous peoples have played
in their own life journey

Discoverers
tell Indigenous stories
Ancestor stories
resistance stories
life stories
without informed permission
without benefits-sharing
taking ownership
of Indigenous knowledges

Discoverers
treat Indigenous lives
cultures
histories
joy and pain
as their source material
or their lightbulb moment

The fourth set of behaviours
belong to the genuine allies
of Indigenous peoples
the change-makers

Change-makers
inform themselves
act according to standards
actively look for bias

especially within themselves
and having found it
do something about it

Change-makers
step off stages
out of spotlights
support Indigenous peoples
to enter the places
from which we've been excluded
support Indigenous peoples
to realise our aspirations
but without claiming credit
for Indigenous success
because change-makers know
it does not belong to them

Change-makers understand
that colonisers occupy space
and decolonisers yield it

PATHWAYS

Humility

Humility is not a feeling
it is a standard
by which to assess your actions
A guiding star
by which to navigate
the complexities of building respectful relationships
with Indigenous peoples
Indigenous sovereignties
on stolen land

Humility means
not stepping in
to Indigenous spaces
conversations
but instead first asking
whether you should be there at all
and if Indigenous peoples
invite you in
asking yourself
what is a respectful way to contribute?
These questions
are not to be asked once
but over and over
Walking humbly
means walking slowly
considering
every step
every gesture
every word
every impact

shifting your pace
to respect Indigenous contexts
to adapt to Indigenous contexts
not expecting
Indigenous contexts to adapt to you

Humility means
understanding that words
ideas
about Indigenous peoples
have a weight and a cost
but if you are not Indigenous
that weight is not one you carry
that cost is not one you pay
which means
you cannot judge the weight
assess the cost
only Indigenous peoples
can do that

Humility
means taking responsibility
for your own learning
doing your best
to be as informed as possible
knowing
that you'll still make mistakes
because no one can ever understand
Indigenous cultures

knowledges
realities
as Indigenous peoples do

Humility means
acknowledging mistakes
not in a way
that burdens Indigenous peoples
with making you feel better
but in a way
that demands nothing of Indigenous peoples
only of yourself

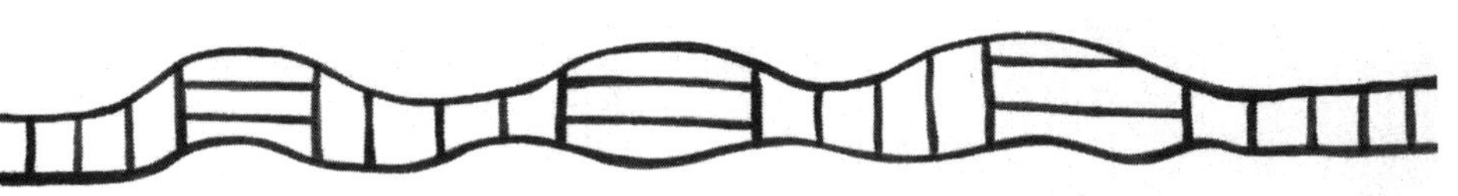

Listening

Listening
can be an act
of transformative power
provided
it is done right

Listening
means understanding silences
Sometimes Settlers think
that where there are silences
about Indigenous peoples
it is the role of Settlers
to fill the quiet
But ask yourself
is there really a silence?
Are Indigenous peoples speaking
and not being heard?
Do Indigenous peoples want to speak
but have no opportunities?
Your role is not to occupy the silence
it is to celebrate
draw attention to
the Indigenous voices already speaking
Or it is to call out the barriers
of settler-colonialism
that prevent
Indigenous voices from speaking

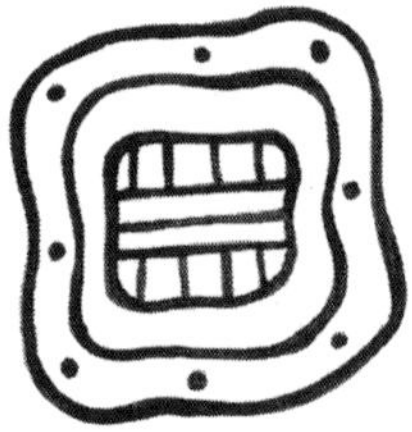

Another kind of silence
is where Indigenous peoples
are choosing not to speak
This can be
for many reasons
including
because knowledge is sacred
restricted
To protect culture
from being misappropriated
or because there are some things
too painful to speak of
This kind of silence
should be respected
remembering
that sometimes silence also speaks

Listening
means understanding
that no one can listen to Indigenous peoples
while telling us
what we want
what is best for us
who we are
or who we should be

Listening
means learning to hear
the noise of settler-colonialism
inside your head

and all around you
so you can hear past it
to understand our voices
on our own terms

Listening means
you can hear the word no
not only hear it
but look for it
be alert
to all the ways Indigenous peoples are showing
we are uncomfortable with sharing

Settler-colonialism
is a serial violator
of Indigenous boundaries
Of lands
bodies
hearts
minds
we are continually pressured
to share
continually involved
in Settler processes
that don't offer the choice
of saying no
such as heritage processes
where we are asked to speak
of sacred things
to have any chance of cultural protection

even though
culture often doesn't get protected
anyway

Listening means
giving time and space
for Indigenous peoples to decide
what we want to share
on what terms we want to share it
or if we want to share at all

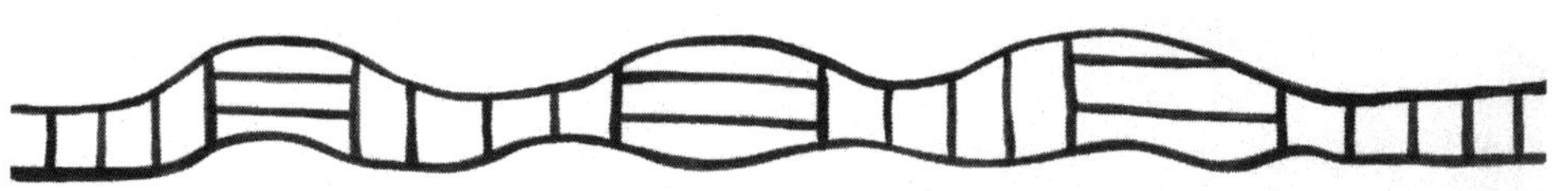

Ask how not what

Many Settlers
ask what can be done
to support Indigenous peoples
But there are many 'whats'
many initiatives
ideas
The only people who can tell you
which ones are right
for which homelands
are the sovereign Indigenous peoples
it is for them to say
what's right for them
what's right for their Country

The 'how'
is as important
often more important
than the 'what'
Things that have been helpful
in one place
might not be appropriate
in another
Things that are good ideas
will fail
if implemented
in disrespectful ways
Thinking about the 'how'
focuses Settler attention
on respectful processes
culturally meaningful

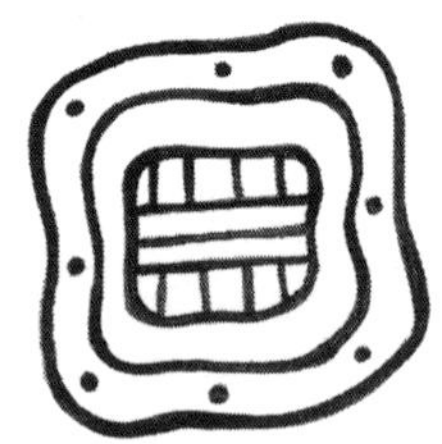

to Indigenous peoples
It is through these processes
enacted through local contexts
answerable to local peoples
that decolonisation
can begin

Here are some
of the basic questions
to be asked
of any project:

Is it Indigenous owned and led?
Is it an equitable partnership
between Indigenous peoples and Settlers?
Is there two-way learning
two-way capacity building
and benefits-sharing
commensurate with the great value
Indigenous peoples bring?

Is it evidence-based
and does that evidence
centre the voices and experiences
of Indigenous peoples?

Is Indigenous involvement
on the basis
of free prior and informed consent?

Free
means free from all pressure
including the pressure
of time
Indigenous peoples are always being asked
to do things
review things
contribute to things
at the last minute
or without enough time
for Indigenous decision-making processes
for proper reflection
consensus
This kind of asking
is a manifestation of discovery doctrine
in the form of the belief
that Indigenous peoples exist
to serve Settler priorities
Often these priorities
have been determined
in the absence of talking
with Indigenous peoples
and even when there has been consultation
what Settlers think is urgent
might not be the most important thing
we are dealing with right now

Prior
means before anything happens
not once a project has started
and if something changes
then this has to be talked about
asked about
agreed to
before any change can be implemented

Informed
is a shared clear understanding
about all aspects of an initiative
including
the benefits to be shared
the best practice ethical standards
to be followed
and the risks
such as the dangers
of misuse or misappropriation
of Indigenous cultural knowledges
and how those dangers will be addressed
by making sure knowledge
is Indigenous owned and controlled

Finally
is the initiative strengths-based?
Too many projects
laws
policies
frameworks

have been based in deficit discourses
which situate Indigenous peoples
as a problem to be solved
by Settler Australia

A strengths-based approach
recognises
the great gifts
resilience
knowledges
of Indigenous peoples
And seeks to build upon
celebrate
utilise
these strengths

A strengths-based approach
recognises
that the cause of Indigenous disadvantage
is dispossession
and all that was done
to achieve it
sustain it
justify it
We are not a problem to be solved
we are partners on pathways
to all the knowledges
inventions

joys
wonders
that will come out of
respectful relationships

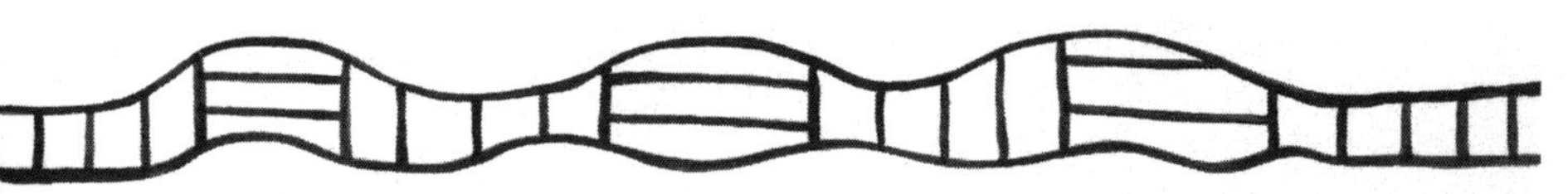

Futures

The places
where different worlds meet
can be places of connection
enrichment and transformation

What is to come
all the things that are next
lives within
the hearts
minds
hopes
of Indigenous peoples
and of Settlers
who are committed
to justice

Decolonised futures
are what we create
together

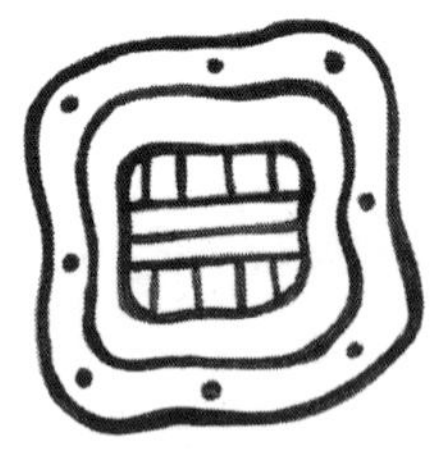

Other titles from Magabala Books

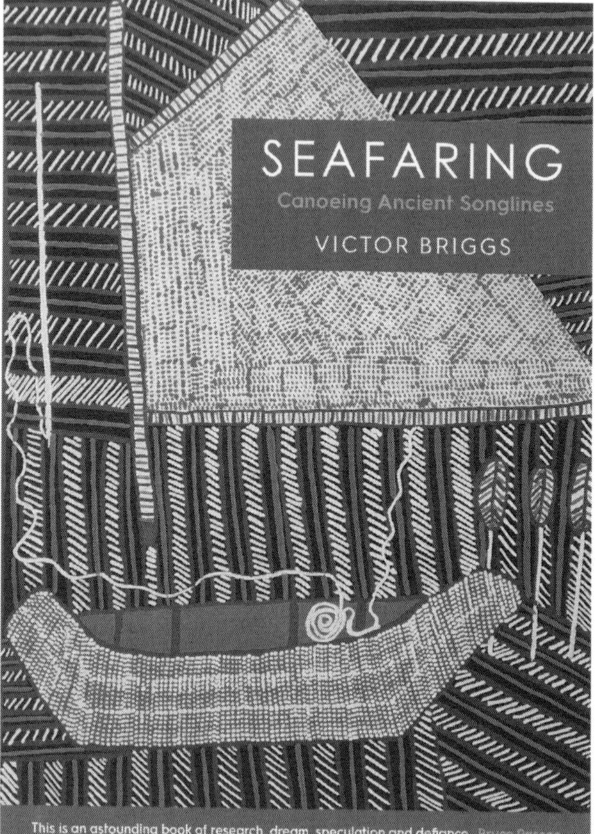
SEAFARING
Canoeing Ancient Songlines
VICTOR BRIGGS
This is an astounding book of research, dream, speculation and defiance. Bruce Pascoe

An ancient story for our time
GURAWUL
THE WHALE
MAX DULUMUNMUN HARRISON
Illustrations Laura La Rosa

YORNADAIYN WOOLAGOODJA

'Wandjina has no mouth because the sound of beginning cannot be heard by human ears.'

Original creation and the renewal of nature
YORRO
YORRO
DAVID MOWALJARLAI & JUTTA MALNIC

BLAKWORK
winner
PRIME MINISTER'S LITERARY AWARDS
SHORTLIST
Victorian Premier's Literary Awards 2019
Shortlist
ALISON WHITTAKER

Close to the Subject
Selected Works
Daniel Browning

Us
Women,
Our
Ways,
Our
World
Edited by Pat Dudgeon, Jeannie Herbert,
Jill Milroy and Darlene Oxenham